FACT CAT

SOUND

Izzi Howell

FACT CAT

Get your paws on this fantastic new
mega-series from Wayland!

Join our Fact Cat on a journey of fun
learning about every subject under the sun!

Published in Great Britain in paperback in 2018 by
Wayland

MIX
Paper from
responsible sources
FSC® C104740

Wayland
An imprint of Hachette Children's Group
Part of Hodder & Stoughton
Carmelite House
50 Victoria Embankment
London EC4Y 0DZ

An Hachette UK Company
www.hachette.co.uk
www.hachettechildrens.co.uk

A catalogue for this title is available from

Picture and illustration credits:
iStock: franckreporter 4, VladimirFLoyd 8, andresr 12;
Shutterstock: worradirek cover, Val Thoermer title page
and 10, nthomas10 5t, adriaticfoto 5b, Darren Pullman 6,
Dmitry Kalinovsky 7, muratart 11, Africa Studio 13, Valentin
Gaina 15, Dieter Hawlan 16, GagliardiImages 17t, Designua
17b, Trofimov Denis 18, Kamira 19, In Green 20, Ivan Kuzmin
21; Stefan Chabluk: 9 and 14.

Every effort has been made to clear copyright.
Should there be any inadvertent omission,
please apply to the publisher for rectification.

**The author, Izzi Howell, is a writer and editor
specialising in children's educational publishing.**

**The consultant, Karina Philip, is a teacher and
a primary literacy consultant with an MA
in creative writing.**

FACT CAT FACT

There is a question for you
to answer on most spreads
in this book. You can check
your answers on page 24.

CONTENTS

WHAT IS SOUND?

Sounds are everywhere. Some are high, such as the cry of a baby. Others are low, such as the sound of thunder.

Fireworks make a very loud sound.

FACT CAT FACT

Hearing is one of the five senses that help us to understand the world. Can you name two of the other senses?

We **communicate** using sounds when we talk to each other.

Most people can hear sounds with their ears. However, some people are deaf, which means that they can't hear much or can't hear at all.

Some deaf people use **sign language** to communicate, instead of talking. These people are using British Sign Language.

the sign for 'perfect'

the sign for 'fantastic'

MAKING SOUNDS

Sounds are made when objects **vibrate** (move back and forth very quickly). These vibrations make **invisible** sound waves that travel through the air to our ears.

When you ring a bell, the metal vibrates and sends out sound waves into the air.

FACT CAT FACT

If you put your hand on your throat while you speak, you can feel the vibrations that are made.

Sound waves can travel through many different materials. As well as **gases**, such as air, they can also move through **solid** objects, such as walls, or **liquids**, such as water.

This man is wearing **foam** headphones, which stop loud sound waves from the drill reaching his ears. Sound does not travel well through foam.

THE EAR

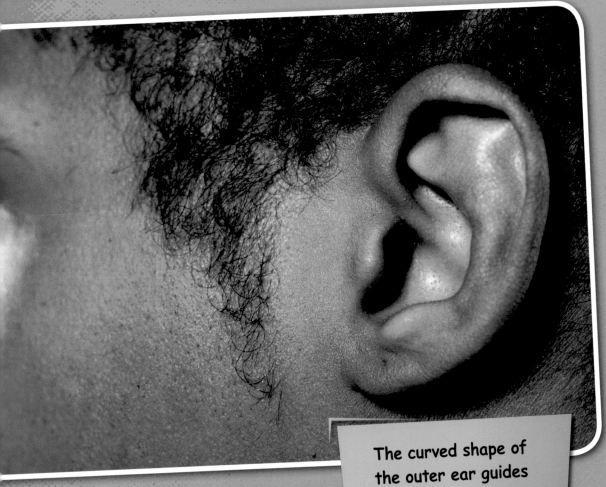

Humans have large, flat **outer ears**. This means that sound waves are more likely to hit them.

The curved shape of the outer ear guides sound waves inside the head. Why does placing an open hand behind your ear help it to catch more sounds?

Inside the ear, sound waves travel to the **eardrum** and make it vibrate. These vibrations pass on to the **middle ear** and the **inner ear**, before travelling to the brain. The brain understands these vibrations as sound.

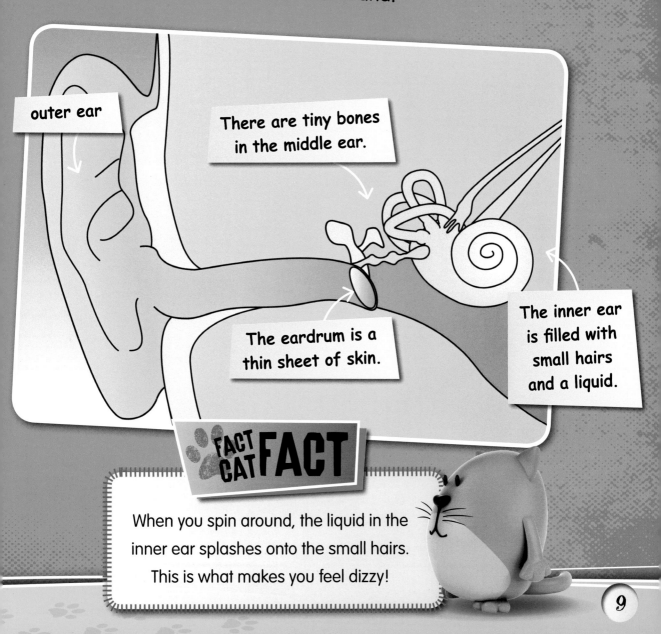

outer ear

There are tiny bones in the middle ear.

The eardrum is a thin sheet of skin.

The inner ear is filled with small hairs and a liquid.

FACT CAT FACT

When you spin around, the liquid in the inner ear splashes onto the small hairs. This is what makes you feel dizzy!

VOLUME

Volume is how loud or quiet a sound is. The stronger the vibrations made by an object, the louder the sound will be.

If you hit a drum hard, it will have strong vibrations and make a loud noise. What kind of sound will it make if you hit it softly?

Sounds that are made far away from you sound quieter than nearby sounds. This is because sound waves lose energy as they travel.

Even loud noises, such as the take-off of a plane, will sound quiet if you are far away.

FACT CAT FACT

The explosion of the Krakatoa volcano in 1883 made such a loud sound that people could still hear it over 4,500 km away!

PITCH

The **pitch** of a sound is how high or low it is. High pitched sounds are made when an object vibrates quickly. Low pitched sounds are made by slow vibrations.

Adult men have lower voices than women. This is because the vibrations made by their voices are slow. Are children's voices high or low?

You can see how pitch works with an elastic band. If you stretch the band loosely across your fingers and **pluck** it, it vibrates slowly. This makes a low sound.

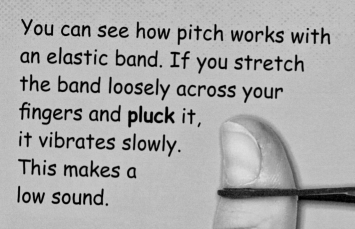

If you pluck a tight band, it will vibrate quickly, which makes a high sound.

FACT CAT FACT

Very high-pitched noises can occasionally break glass!

REFLECTING SOUND

When you make a noise, sound waves move away from you. If the sound waves hit a hard object, some of the sound bounces back towards you.

When sound waves hit a soft surface, the surface **absorbs** the waves.

This diagram shows how sound is **reflected** when sound waves hit a hard surface.

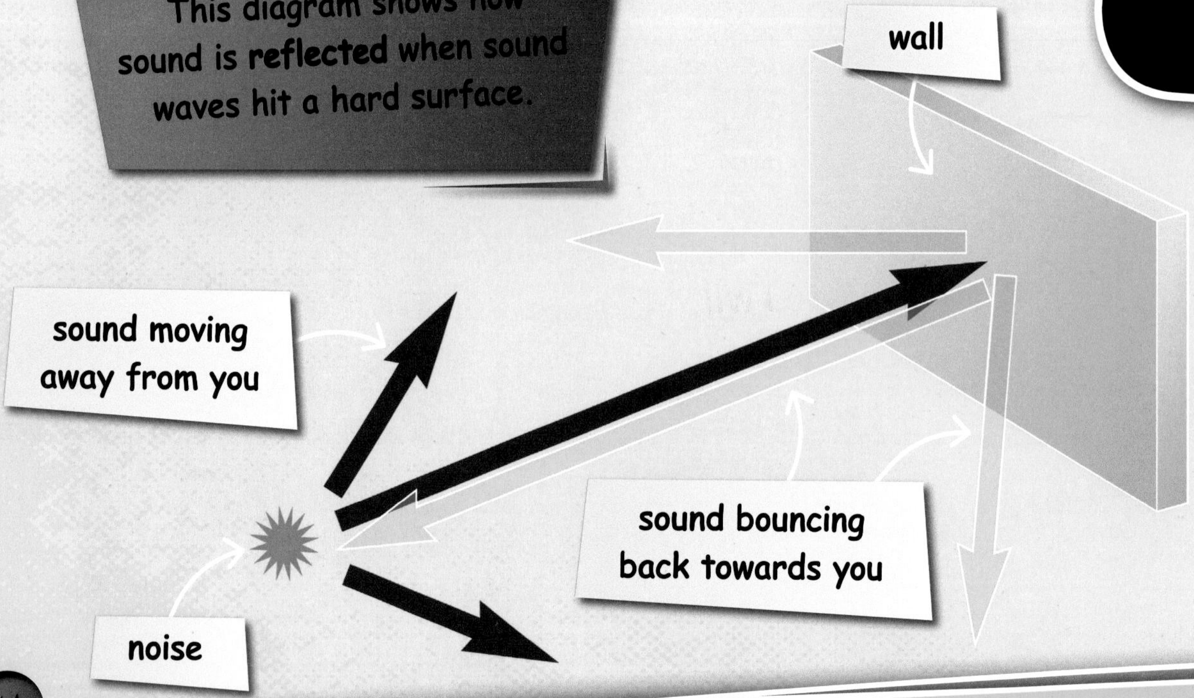

wall

sound moving away from you

sound bouncing back towards you

noise

If you are far enough away from the hard surface, you will hear an **echo** (repeated sound) when the sound bounces back. If you are too close, the sound and the echo will happen at the same time.

You often hear echoes in caves because sound bounces off the hard cave walls. Can you think of another place where echoes are common?

USING SOUNDS

We mainly use sound for communication but sound can also tell us about our **surroundings**. We can hear if it's raining or if someone is walking towards us.

When crossing the road, it's important to listen for traffic as well as looking both ways.

FACT CAT FACT

We know the direction that a sound comes from because the ear closest to the sound sends a message to the brain.

We can also use sound waves to find things that are hidden underwater or inside the body. This works by sending out sound waves that are reflected back when they hit an object.

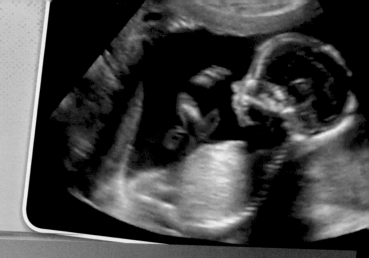

This is an image of an unborn baby inside the body of its mother. It is made by sending very high-pitched sounds, known as ultrasound, into the body.

sound waves

This diagram shows how sonar works. Sonar is a way of using sound to find underwater objects. Why is sonar useful for fishermen?

MUSICAL INSTRUMENTS

Musical instruments make sounds in different ways. **Percussion** instruments, such as drums, make sounds when you hit them. String instruments, such as guitars and violins, make sound when their strings vibrate.

Guitar strings vibrate and make sounds when they are plucked by fingers. What does a violin player use to make the strings vibrate?

Wind instruments vibrate and make sounds when a musician blows air into them. Some examples of wind instruments are the flute, the recorder and the trumpet.

This musician can change or note, that the trumpet pressing the

ANIMALS AND SOUND

Some animals, such as rabbits, have excellent hearing. They need to hear if danger is coming so that they can run away and stay safe.

Dogs can hear ultrasound noises that humans can't. This is why dogs react to ultrasound dog whistles that we can't hear.

Dolphins use a type of sonar called **echolocation** to find food. They send out ultrasound clicking sounds, which reflect off fish and travel back to the dolphin. The dolphin then swims towards the fish to catch it.

FACT CAT FACT

Whales communicate with each other by making different sounds. Their sounds can travel for thousands of kilometres underwater.

Bats also use echolocation to find their way around in the dark. Find out the name of another animal that uses echolocation.

QUIZ

Try to answer the questions below. Look back through the book to help you. Check your answers on page 24.

1 Hearing is one of the five senses. True or not true?

a) true

b) not true

2 Which part of the ear is not inside your head?

a) eardrum

b) middle ear

c) outer ear

3 Strong vibrations make quiet sounds. True or not true?

a) true

b) not true

4 Sound bounces off soft surfaces. True or not true?

a) true

b) not true

5 Which type of instrument is a flute?

a) percussion

b) wind

c) string

6 Which animal uses echolocation?

a) dolphin

b) cat

c) pigeon

GLOSSARY

absorb to take something in

communicate to share information with others

eardrum a thin sheet of skin inside your ear

echo a sound made by the reflection of sound waves off of a surface, which causes you to hear a sound twice

echolocation the way in which some animals use ultrasound to find their way around or to find food

foam a soft, squishy material

gas something that is neither a solid nor a liquid, such as air

inner ear a part of your ear inside your head that sends signals about sound to the brain

invisible describes something or someone that can't be seen

liquid something that is neither a solid nor a gas, such as milk

middle ear a part of your ear inside your head that passes vibrations to the inner ear

outer ear the part of your ear that is on the outside of your head

percussion a type of musical instrument that makes a sound when you hit it

pitch how high or low a sound is

pluck to pull with your fingers

reflect if something reflects light, it sends the light back and does not absorb it

sign language a language that uses hand movements, often used by deaf people

solid something that is neither a liquid nor a gas, such as a table

sonar a system that uses sound waves to find underwater objects

surroundings the things and conditions around a person or thing

ultrasound very high pitched sound waves

vibrate to move back and forth very quickly

INDEX

ANSWERS

Pages 4–21

Page 4: The five senses are hearing, sight, touch, taste and smell.

Page 8: It makes the ear larger and more curved, meaning that more sound waves will hit the ear and be guided inside.

Page 10: Quiet

Page 12: High

Page 15: Some places include tunnels and empty halls.

Page 17: They know where they will be able to catch fish.

Page 18: A bow

Page 21: Killer whales, porpoises and shrews use echolocation.

Quiz answers

1   true

2   c – outer ear

3   not true – weak vibrations make quiet sounds.

4   not true – sound is absorbed by soft surfaces.

5   b – wind

6   a – dolphin